Me!

Self-Awareness & Self-Esteem

World Teachers Press®
www.worldteacherspress.com

Published with the permission of R.I.C. Publications Pty. Ltd.

Copyright © 2006 by Didax, Inc., Rowley, MA 01969. All rights reserved.

First published by R.I.C. Publications Pty. Ltd., Perth, Western Australia. Revised by Didax Educational Resources.

Limited reproduction permission: The publisher grants permission to individual teachers who have purchased this book to reproduce the blackline masters as needed for use with their own students. Reproduction for an entire school or school district or for commercial use is prohibited.

Printed in the United States of America.

Order Number 2-5244
ISBN 978-1-58324-212-4

B C D E F 10 09 08 07 06

395 Main Street
Rowley, MA 01969
www.didax.com

Foreword

Me! is a comprehensive book of motivating activities designed for early learners discovering what makes them special as they interact and become part of a community.

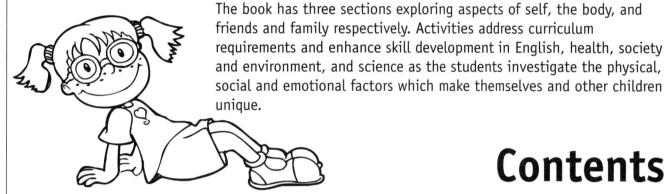

The book has three sections exploring aspects of self, the body, and friends and family respectively. Activities address curriculum requirements and enhance skill development in English, health, society and environment, and science as the students investigate the physical, social and emotional factors which make themselves and other children unique.

Contents

Teacher Notes

Me! investigates topics most suited to students developing an awareness of self and their relationships with others. Activities will interest students of varying ability levels and will enhance learning in a range of lower elementary class themes.

The activities included aim to develop three distinct concepts:

*   self-awareness and self-esteem (All About Me)
*   exploring the body and what it can do (My Body)
*   people we interact with (My Family and Friends)

"All About Me" includes:

*   identifying individual qualities and abilities
*   how we grow and change
*   where we live
*   making good decisions
*   needs and wants
*   encouraging individual potential

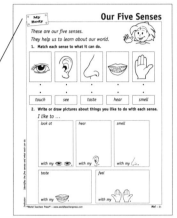

"My Body" provides opportunities for students to:

*   identify body parts
*   explore the senses
*   investigate good eating and exercise practices for keeping the body healthy

"My Family and Friends" identifies:

*   people we are related to
*   roles and responsibilities in the family
*   considering others
*   the qualities which make good friendships

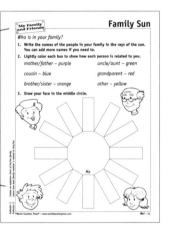

An indicator has been written down the side of each activity to assist you in focusing your accompanying lesson appropriately. This indicator can also be used in the assessment outline provided on page 5 should you choose to use a "Me!" activity as a student work sample.

Using the Assessment Outline

An explanation of how to use the assessment outline on page 5 is detailed below.

Fill in the appropriate learning area.

Give a brief description of the activities in the chosen worksheet and what was expected of the students.

Write the relevant outcome(s) of the task.

List the indicator(s) assessed on the chosen worksheet.

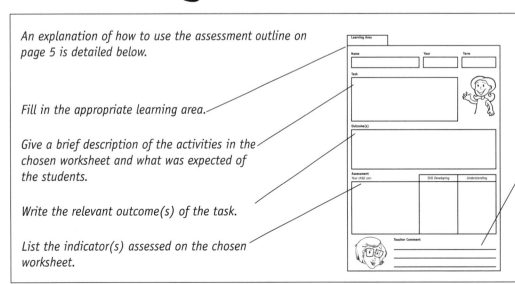

Use this space to comment on an individual student's performance which can not be indicated in the formal assessment, such as work habits or particular needs or abilities.

 ©World Teachers Press® ~ www.worldteacherspress.com

Learning Area

Assessment Outline

Name

Grade

Term

Task

Outcome(s)

Assessment

Your child can:

	Still Developing	Understanding

Teacher Comment

_____

_____

_____

Me! ~ 5

Overview

The Arts

Music and Movement
- Sings songs about "me," such as "When You're Happy and You Know It."
- Works through fingerplays and songs about body movements.
- Students move to music facing a partner, mirroring each other's movements.
- Use musical instruments to copy the syllable rhythm of students' first names and surnames.
- Play some different pieces of classical music while students lie down with their eyes closed. Discuss which was each student's favorite and why.

Arts and Crafts
- Allow each student to paint a self-portrait on a large sheet of paper. When dry, cut around the painting, leaving a narrow unpainted border, and display.
- Students create their own shield, dividing it into a favorite book, food and toy.
- Trace around a body and use collage materials to decorate and display. Extend by making a front and back shape and decorate and fill with crushed newspaper to pad out the shape.
- Use finger, hand, or footprints to create mini-creatures or designs.
- Paint and frame "Me and My Family" pictures.
- Students decorate their names in bright bold patterns and shapes.
- Use a mirror to help paint or draw a self-portrait. Display without names to see if other students can guess the identity.

Dance and Drama
- Make up dance movements which focus on different parts of the body.
- Move to the "Hokey Pokey."
- Role-play situations that make students happy, sad, angry, worried, etc.
- Students experiment with voice, movements and facial expressions to create individual characters.

English

Speaking and Listening
- Encourage each student to share news about his or her life.
- Students describe what they would like to do when they grow up and why they would like to do it.
- Students say one true and one false sentence about themselves. Class must decide which is the truth.
- Write and present poetry or songs about the five senses.
- Students sit in a circle. One student makes a statement. If the statement is true for other students, they stand up. For example, "My favorite food is corn," "I love to play soccer."
- Students bring a small box of treasured things and discuss their importance with the class.
- Have a "Student of the Week" describe himself/herself and his/her likes and dislikes. Written information is displayed about the student for the week.
- Make up interview questions for a family survey about each member's favorite things.

Reading and Viewing
- Read about different families and compare them to students' families.
- Read stories which explore issues such as sharing, caring for others, being special and friendship.
- View photographs showing the same people getting older.
- Read "The Popcorn Book" by Tomie de Paola to review the senses involved in making popcorn.
- Cut out pictures of people from magazines and make up personal details such as name, family, home, etc. This can be done orally or written as a character profile.

Writing
- Write an "I ..." book, describing "Who I Am," "What I Have" and "What I Like."
- Discuss favorite foods, then write recipes for them using a writing framework.
- Write about a special place. Why is it special? Who shares your special place?
- Write an acrostic poem from first name letters.
- Students use their senses to describe and write about the object inside a "mystery box."
- Students develop rhyming sentences to go with their names.
- Students complete sentences about themselves. For example, "I am a good friend because ...," "I am the greatest at ..."
- Students design a "Wanted" or "Lost" poster about themselves.
- Construct a "Can You Guess?" book. Students describe themselves and others read and try to guess their identity.
- Design a merit award for something each student was proud to achieve.

Word Study
- Each student writes words describing himself/herself on strips of colored paper and glues them to a self-portrait.
- Develop a class list of things students can do, such as jump, clap, hop, chew, wiggle, etc. Refer to the list when playing music and movement games.
- List "emotion" words and write synonyms.
- Look at words related to the senses; e.g. sight, see, ear, touch, etc.
- Sort students' names into boys, girls, alphabetical order, number of letters, initial consonants, syllables, etc.

Media
- Videotape students in class and on the playground. View the video while students explain the activities.
- Find pictures in magazines of things we need. Glue them into quadrants labeled "food," "shelter," "clothing" and "love."
- Record an interview with an older person about his/her schooldays and home life. Students compare with their own.

©World Teachers Press® ~ www.worldteacherspress.com

Mathematics

Working Mathematically/
Appreciating Mathematics
- *Sort students' shoes or schoolbags in various ways.*
- *Plan an exercise routine.*
- *Discuss the different kinds of mathematics that could be involved with the body; e.g. measurement, counting, area.*

Space
- *Students in pairs take turns giving each other directions while one is blindfolded.*
- *Explore positional terms and have students move to the appropriate places; e.g. under the table, beside the chalkboard.*
- *Have students explore symmetrical and asymmetrical positions by making different shapes with their bodies.*
- *Trace around each student. Use blocks to measure and compare the area of each. Include half-block and quarter-block measurements.*
- *Use a variety of 2-D shapes to construct a person.*

Measurement
- *Use body parts to measure lengths.*
- *Develop a list of activities that take about a minute each for students to do.*
- *Compare heights of students using standard measures.*
- *Use paper streamers to measure body parts and make a paper skeleton.*
- *Bring a favorite toy to school to measure.*
- *Fill in times on clock faces of when students go to bed, get up, eat lunch, etc.*

Chance and Data
- *Play "Build a Person" by spinning for body parts to build up a person.*
- *Graph the physical features, likes and dislikes of class members using colored bricks or a pictograph wall chart and compare the results.*
- *Construct a birthday pictograph for each month. Write names on "birthday cakes" with the correct number of candles. Students color the candles when their birthday occurs.*

Number
- *Reinforce equal and unequal sharing by providing concrete materials for students to share with others.*
- *Construct number stories about "me," e.g. "I have 3 dolls and 4 ponies. I have 7 toys altogether."*
- *In pairs, trace numbers and simple equations on each other's backs. Take turns to guess.*
- *Stare at a partner and count how many times he or she blinks in a set time.*
- *Count in ones, twos, etc. to discover how many shoes, socks, hands, fingers, ears, etc. are in the class.*

Health and Physical Education

- *Build a tower of covered boxes with the names of things which help us grow.*
- *Investigate activities which keep us fit and strong. Hold a carnival with events the students devise.*
- *Ask students to undertake a variety of activities and identify which part of the body is being exercised; e.g. arms, neck, legs, feet.*
- *Discuss what "being healthy" means and what we can do to stay healthy.*

Science

- *Use a model of the human body which can be disassembled to show its parts.*
- *Identify and locate parts of the body, including sense organs.*
- *Discuss the differences between humans and other animals.*
- *Explain the difference between living and non-living things in terms of characteristics like movement and growth.*
- *Investigate genetic traits in families; e.g. tongue rolling, dimples, eye color.*
- *Look at fingerprints and discuss differences between individuals.*
- *Label diagrams of the ear, eye and teeth. Write descriptive sentences.*

Studies of Society and Environment

- *Bring an item of baby or toddler clothing each student used to wear to show how people grow and change.*
- *Hold a "special talents" day for students to showcase sporting, artistic, or musical talents.*
- *Investigate the lifestyles of children in other parts of the world and compare them to students' lifestyles.*
- *Describe changes in students since birth. Draw a time line that represents events in their lives to date.*
- *Construct family trees.*
- *Compile lists of rules students are expected to follow at school and home. Discuss.*
- *Discuss and draw what each student might do and look like as a teenager, older person, etc.*

Technology and Enterprise

- *Have each student select objects from the classroom that make him/her feel safe and happy at school. Students then use these items to design a special "nook" they would like to use at school.*
- *Design a time capsule. Students choose four things to be placed in the capsule and explain to the class why they have chosen these items.*
- *Students design a new house/building for their family.*

How Do I Look?

All About Me

1. **Draw a portrait of yourself in the picture frame.**
2. **Finish the sentences.**

   (a) My hair is | brown | blonde | black | red | gray |.

   (b) My eyes are | green | brown | blue | hazel | gray |.

   (c) My chin is | round | oval | square | pointy |.

   (d) My body is | short | tall | medium |.

   (e) My hair is | long | short | spiky | curly | straight |.

   (f) My skin is | fair | dark | tanned | freckly |.

©World Teachers Press® ~ www.worldteacherspress.com

Indicator: *Identifies features of his/her physical appearance.*

Something I take care of

The thing I do best

My proudest moment

My best quality

I am

A good deed I've done

People like me because ...

My closest friends

A way I help others

My "happy" place

Indicator: *Identifies and appreciates positive personal qualities.*

My House

Where do you live? What is your phone number?
It is very important to know this information in case of
an emergency.

1. **Write your phone number on the telephone.**

2. **Write your address on the mailbox.**

My phone number is ...

My address is...

Sometimes people have an
emergency in their home and
need to call for help.

3. **Write some reasons you might**
    need to call for help.

_____

_____

_____

4. **Write the emergency phone**
    number.

EMERGENCY
Phone Number

Indicator: *Recalls important phone numbers and home address details.*

©World Teachers Press® ~ www.worldteacherspress.com

As we grow up there are more and more things we can do. Look at the time line. Think of things you could do for each box. Draw pictures for each.

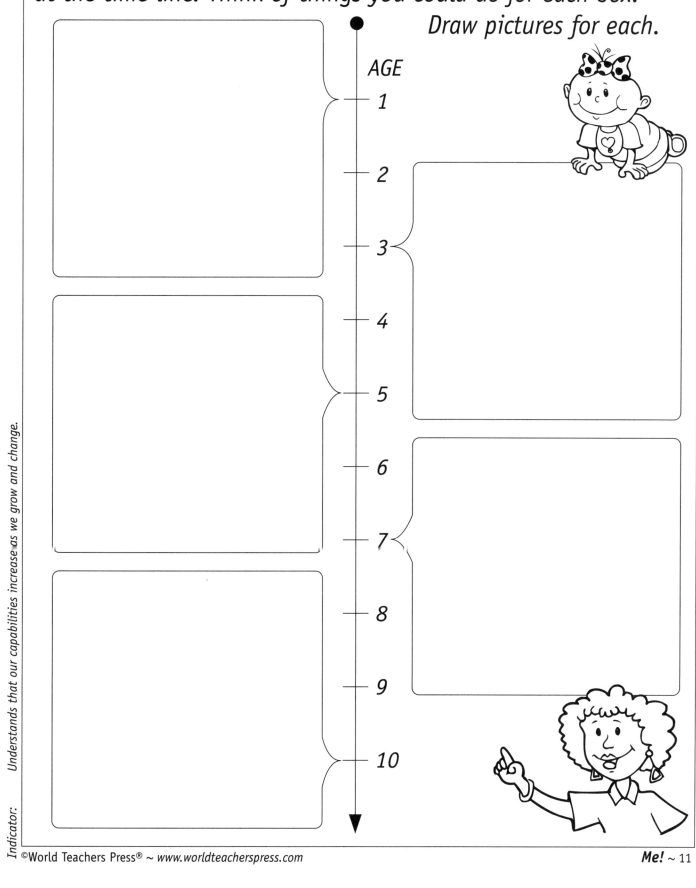

Indicator: Understands that our capabilities increase as we grow and change.

My Favorite Things

List **your** favorite things!

_____

_____

_____

_____

_____

_____

©World Teachers Press® ~ www.worldteacherspress.com

Magnificent Me!

Read the poem "Magnificent Me." Use the guide below to write your own "Magnificent Me" poem!

Magnificent Me!

Do you know Magnificent Me?
Read my poem and you will see ...
I am happy.
And I am cool.
I like running.
And I like the beach.
My friends are Richie,
And Marly and Maddy.
I can swim,
And I can dance.
I'm as clever as can be.
Because I am ...
Magnificent Me!

Magnificent Me

Do you know Magnificent Me?
Read my poem and you will see ...

I am _____ ,

And I am _____ .

I like _____ ,

And I like _____ .

My friends are _____ ,

And _____ *and* _____ .

I can _____ ,

And I can _____ .

I'm as clever as can be,

Because I am ...

Magnificent Me!

Indicator: Uses a set model to write a poem about self.

Things I Need and Things I Want

Needs are things we must have to stay alive. All people have four types of needs. They are **food**, **shelter**, **clothing** and **love**. Draw a picture for each type of **need**.

Wants are things we wish we could have but don't need to keep us alive. Different people want different things. Draw four of the things you **want**.

©World Teachers Press® ~ www.worldteacherspress.com

Look What I Can Do!

Look! I can write my name!

When I am on the
playground,
I can do this!

I am _____

_____ .

Draw

Draw

I can be a good helper!

I can _____

_____ .

I can be a good friend!

I _____

_____ .

Draw

Indicator: Identifies things they can do.

©World Teachers Press® ~ www.worldteacherspress.com

My Talents

Some people are good at sports. Some people are good at music.
Everybody is good at something.
Some people are good at lots of things!

When we go to school, we get to try
many things to find out what we are good at.

1. **Draw some new things you have tried
    since you have been at school.**

2. **Were you good at any of the things you drew?**   Yes / No

    *You can practice doing things to
    become good at them.*

3. **What is something you would
    like to be really good at?**

    _____

    _____

4. **Draw a picture of
    you practicing
    what you would
    like to be good at.**

Indicator: *Understands that people can develop special skills and talents.*

   ©World Teachers Press® ~ www.worldteacherspress.com

One of a Kind

Did you know that there are no two people exactly the same—not even twins?

We have patterns on our skin which make us one of a kind. It's like our own special code!

1. **Make a print of your thumb and four fingers in the boxes. Compare them to other people's prints in your class.**

Thumb	Pointer	Middle	Ring	Pinky

2. **Does anyone have the same fingerprints as you?** Yes / No

   It's good to be different! Lots of things make us different from other people.

3. **Color the boxes which contain things that make you feel different.**

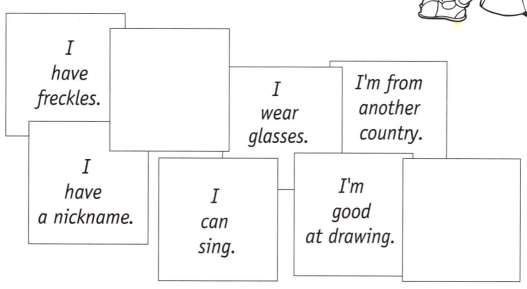

I have freckles.

I have a nickname.

I can sing.

I wear glasses.

I'm from another country.

I'm good at drawing.

4. **In the blank boxes, write two things that make you different.**

Indicator: *Recognizes the things that make us different and special.*

Good Decision!

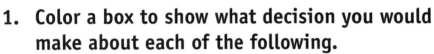

Sometimes it can be hard deciding what to do. People make decisions about what to do every day of their lives. Some decisions are small and others are very important.

1. **Color a box to show what decision you would make about each of the following.**

(a) What will you wear to school tomorrow?

| shorts | skirt | pants |

(b) Who will you play with at lunchtime?

| friends | the teacher | brother or sister |

(c) How will you solve an argument with another student?

| friends | the teacher | brother or sister |

(d) If you had $2.00 to spend at lunchtime, what would you buy?

| ice cream | milk | fruit |

(e) If a stranger starts talking to you, what will you do?

| walk away | talk to him/her | tell an adult |

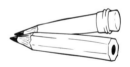

2. **When you are growing up, other people make some decisions for you. Choose a person from the box to write next to the decion he/she makes for you.**

parent   teacher

me   friend

(a) Who I sit next to in class. _____

(b) What I eat for dinner. _____

(c) Who my friends are. _____

(d) What game I play at lunchtime._____

(e) What I wear to school. _____

Makes appropriate decisions when required.

©World Teachers Press® ~ www.worldteacherspress.com

Indicator:

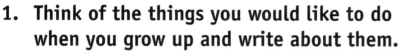
All
About
Me

When I Grow Up

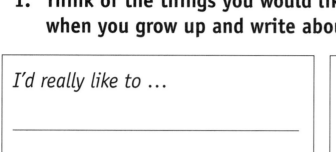

It's fun to imagine what it would be like to be grown up!

1. Think of the things you would like to do when you grow up and write about them.

I'd really like to ...

_____

The best part would be ...

_____

_____

_____

Before I could do this I would need to ...

_____

_____

I'd also like to ...

_____

The best part would be ...

_____

_____

_____

Before I could do this I would need to ...

_____

_____

2. What would be some of the hard things about being a grown-up?

_____

_____

3. Which would you rather be? | *child* | *grown-up* |

Why? _____

Indicator: Imagines what life might be like as an adult.

Body Jigsaw

Can you put this body back together?

1. **Cut out each body part. Glue them onto a piece of paper to make a body.**

2. **Cut out the body words. Use them to label the body.**

3. **Draw hair, eyes, nose, clothes, etc. to make the body look like a person.**

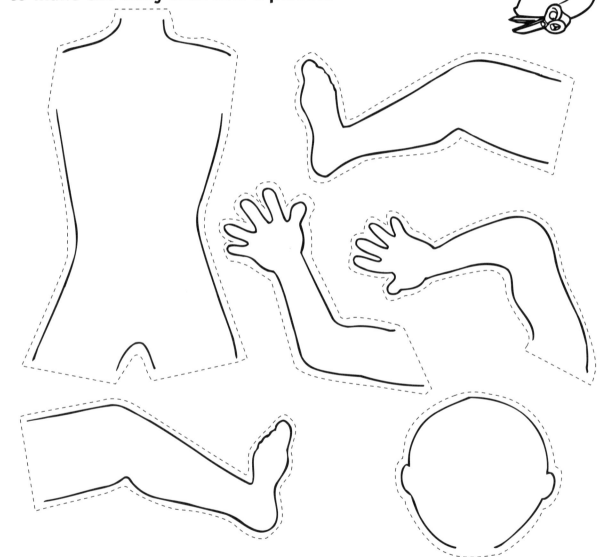

head	foot	arm	neck
leg	stomach	elbow	wrist
knee	hand	shoulder	ankle

Indicator 1: Recognizes parts of the body to construct a jigsaw.
Indicator 2: Matches labels of body parts to a picture.

©World Teachers Press® ~ www.worldteacherspress.com

Our Five Senses

These are our five senses.

They help us to learn about our world.

1. Match each sense to what it can do.

   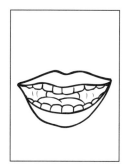 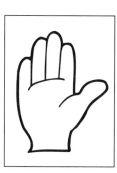

| touch | see | taste | hear | smell |

2. Write or draw pictures about things you like to do with each sense.

I like to ...

| look at | hear | smell |

with my 👀. | with my 👂. | with my 👃.

 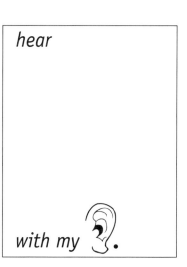 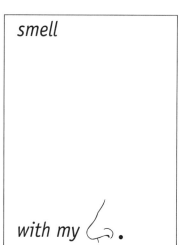

| taste | feel |

with my 👄. | with my ✋✋.

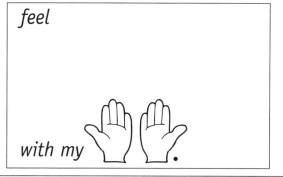

Indicator: Identifies the five senses and what each can do.

©World Teachers Press® ~ www.worldteacherspress.com

My Eyes

You see with your eyes. Use your eyes to help you with these activities.

1. Check eight things that begin with "s."

2. Circle three things that rhyme with "see."

3. Put an X next to three things that end in "sh."

4. Write three things that begin with "fr."

_____   _____   _____

5. Can you find me in the picture?

Indicator: Uses the sense of sight to complete visual discrimination activities.

©World Teachers Press® ~ www.worldteacherspress.com

My Body

You hear with your ears.

Use your ears to help you with these activities.

1. **Draw or write about things you can hear inside and outside your classroom.**

	Inside	*Outside*
Loud		
Soft		

2. **Circle the loud sounds. Check the soft sounds.**

Indicator: Uses the sense of hearing to complete auditory discrimination activities.

My Nose

You smell with your nose.

Use your nose to help you with these activities.

1. **Smell each of these things.**

   Write words to describe how each smells.

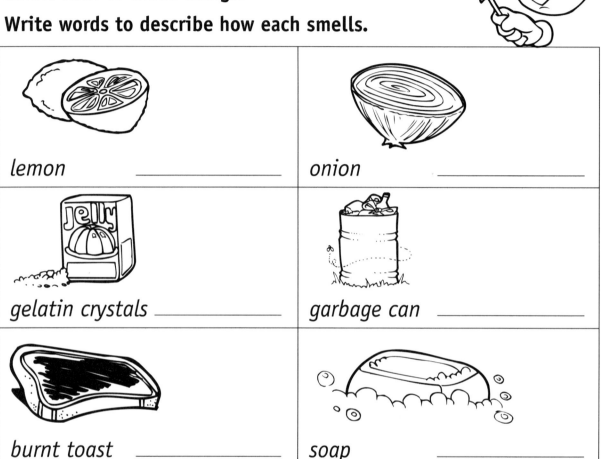

lemon _____	onion _____
gelatin crystals _____	garbage can _____
burnt toast _____	soap _____
tin of fish _____	flower _____

2. **Draw and label one thing you like to smell and one thing you don't like to smell.**

Like	Don't like

Indicator: Uses the sense of smell to describe the smell of a variety of objects.

©World Teachers Press® ~ www.worldteacherspress.com

My Tongue

You taste with your tongue.

Use your tongue to help you with these activities.

1. Taste each of the things below.

Color the box red if it tastes sour.
Color the box yellow if it tastes sweet.
Color the box green if it tastes salty.

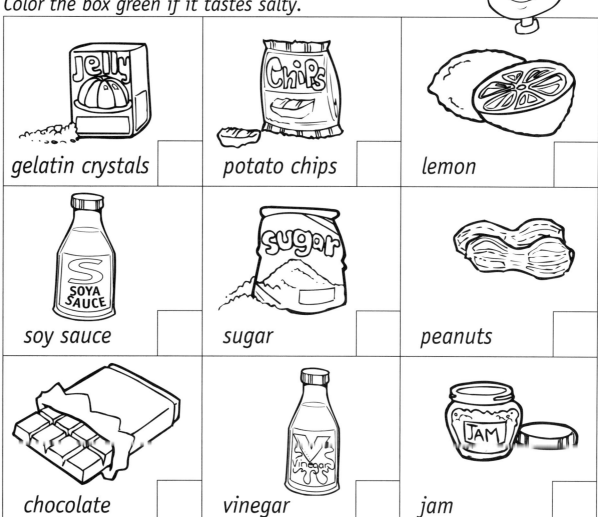

gelatin crystals	potato chips	lemon
soy sauce	sugar	peanuts
chocolate	vinegar	jam

2. Draw something in each box that tastes ...

sour	sweet	salty

Indicator: Uses the sense of taste to distinguish salt, sour, sweet, or strong flavors.

My Hands

You feel or touch things with your hands.

Use your hands to help you with these activities.

1. **Feel each of the things below.**

    Use the words at the bottom of the page or others you can think of to describe how each object felt.

cotton balls	sand	honey	stick

golf ball	water	sandpaper	your cheek

hard	soft	fluffy	wet	dry
smooth	rough	prickly	sticky	pointy

Indicator: Uses the sense of touch to match words to how objects feel.

©World Teachers Press® ~ www.worldteacherspress.com

What Can You Do?

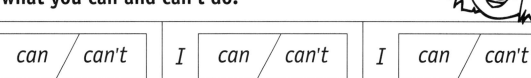

1. Can you do these things with your body?

Color what you can and can't do.

I	can / can't

touch my toes without bending my knees.

I	can / can't

roll my tongue.

I	can / can't

do this with my fingers.

I	can / can't

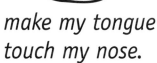

make my tongue touch my nose.

I	can / can't

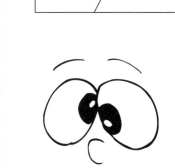
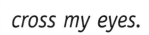

cross my eyes.

I	can / can't

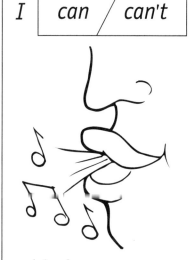

whistle.

2. Draw two more things you can do with your body.

Indicator: *Explores actions his/her body can and can't do.*

Are You Healthy?

There are lots of things you should do to keep your body healthy. You will find out some of these ways on this sheet. Can you think of other ways to stay healthy?

1. Cut out the labels below.   **2. Glue them under the correct picture.**

Indicator: *Recognizes important ways to maintain a healthy body.*

Eat healthy food.	Get plenty of sleep.
Drink lots of water.	Do some exercise.
Keep your body clean.	Visit the dentist and doctor.

©World Teachers Press® ~ www.worldteacherspress.com

Eating and Exercise Diary

Draw or write about the foods you ate and the exercise you did on each day.

Day	Food	Exercise
Monday		
Tuesday		
Wednesday		
Thursday		
Friday		
Saturday		
Sunday		

Indicator: Records foods eaten and exercise completed over a week.

Keeping Your Body Safe

There are lots of things you should do to keep your body safe. You will find out some of these ways on this sheet.

1.   Draw a picture or write about some ways to keep safe.

_____

Don't talk to strangers.

Be careful crossing the road.

_____

_____

Put on sunscreen.

2.   Draw and write about another way to keep safe.

_____

_____

_____

Indicator: Recognizes important ways to keep his/her body safe.

©World Teachers Press® ~ www.worldteacherspress.com

Note: Picture can be used: (1) as a class picture talk, (2) as a barrier game, (3) enlarged and labeled, (4) cut up and used as a jigsaw, or (5) for individual or small groups to discuss healthy/unhealthy foods, types of exercise, safety concerns, etc.

My Family

A family is a group of people.

A family usually has parents and children who live in the same house.

1. Draw a picture of your family and write a name next to each person.

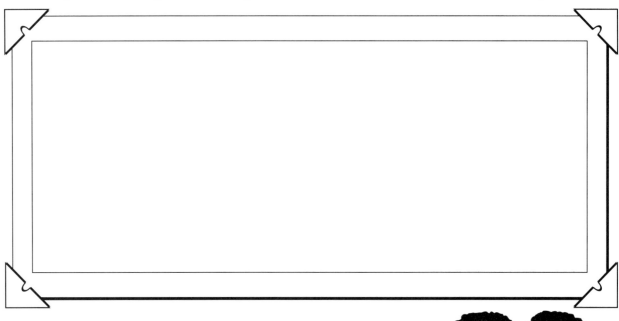

2. Complete the sentences.

(a) *There are _____ people in my family.*

(b) *The number of my house is _____.*

(c) *The name of my street is _____*

_____

(d) *My phone number is _____*

3. (a) *Write your last name in big letters in the box. This is called your family name.*

(b) *Color and make patterns on, in, or around the letters.*

Indicator: Completes information about own family.

©World Teachers Press® ~ www.worldteacherspress.com

Family Sun

Who is in your family?

1. **Write the names of the people in your family in the rays of the sun. You can add more names if you need to.**

2. **Lightly color each box to show how each person is related to you.**

   mother/father – purple   *uncle/aunt – green*

   cousin – blue   *grandparent – red*

   brother/sister – orange   *other – yellow*

3. **Draw your face in the middle circle.**

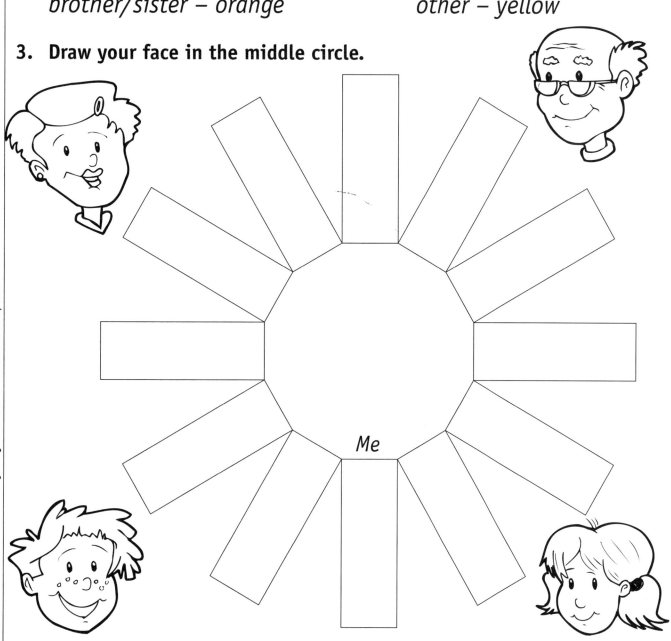

Me

Indicator 1: Creates an explosion chart of his/her family.
Indicator 2: Learns how each family member is related to him/her.

©World Teachers Press® ~ www.worldteacherspress.com

Me! ~ 33

Family Words

Use the words in the word bank to help you answer the questions.

son	daughter	grandparents	brother	father
niece	wife	husband	grandchild	sister
step-parent	aunt	mother	uncle	nephew

1. **Write the words that begin with the word "grand."**

   _____   _____

2. **Write two more words from the word bank you could add to "grand."**

   grandson, _____   _____

3. **Complete the male and female pairs.**

   (a) wife _____   *(c) aunt* _____

   (b) brother _____   *(d) son* _____

4. **Match the sentence beginnings to their correct ending.**

   (a)   A man is married to his   •   •   *niece.*

   (b)   A person's girl child is a   •   •   *daughter.*

   (c)   A woman is aunt to her   •   •   *son.*

   (d)   A person's boy child is a   •   •   *wife.*

5. **Write any special names you call members of your family. For example, you might call your mother "Mom."**

family member	special name

Indicator: Understands the meanings of "family" words.

©World Teachers Press® ~ www.worldteacherspress.com

Different Families

What is a family? It is different for everyone.

Some families have lots of people. Some are very small. Other families have grandparents or other people living with them. Sometimes people from two different families become one.

Imagine your two penpals send you these emails about their families.

Dear penpal,
I live with my mom and dad, sister and my grandma and grandad. We live in a small house with three bedrooms, so my brother and I have to share. We are a noisy and busy family. One thing we like to do together is play music.
From Keenan

Dear penpal,
I used to live with my mom and my brother, but last year Mom got married and now we live with my step-dad and stepsister in their huge house! I like living with my new family. They do exciting things. My step-dad has taught my brother and me how to ride horses and we do this most weekends together.
From Jacob

1. **Write an email in reply about your own family.**

2. **Complete the table.**

	My Family	Keenan	Jacob
number of people			
size of home			
type of family			
do together			

Indicator: Understands that all families are different.

Family Favorites

Interview three people in your family to find out these things

Name			
Favorite TV program			
Are you the oldest or the youngest or somewhere else in the family?			
Favorite food			
Hobbies			
Favorite family celebration			
Favorite sport			

Answer these Questions.

1. Which member of the family is more like you?

   _____

2. Who is least like you?

   _____

3. Did anyone like all the same things as you?

   _____

Indicator: Interviews family members to discover differences and similarities.

©World Teachers Press® ~ www.worldteacherspress.com

Family Homes

Read about these family homes.

Toshi lives in an apartment. It is on the fifth floor of a big building. Her home is made from concrete.

Scott lives in a farmhouse.
It is not near any other houses. His home is made from bricks.

1. **Follow the pattern to write and draw about where you live.**

    I live _____.

    It is _____

    _____.

    My home is made from

    _____.

2. **Answer the questions about your home.**

    (a) *Does your home have a backyard?* $\boxed{Yes / No}$

    (b) *Do you have your own bedroom?* $\boxed{Yes / No}$

    (c) *How many pets do you own?* _____

    (d) *What is your favorite place at home?* _____

3. **Discuss how other people in your class answered these questions.**

Indicator: Reads and compares a range of family homes.

Family Jobs and Rules

People in families help each other by following family rules and sharing jobs around the home.

1. **Write three rules your family has, e.g. bedtime.
    Discuss why you think your family has these rules.**

2. **Write who does these jobs in your family. There may be more than one name for each job. Add more of your own.**

vacuuming		cooking	
gardening		setting the table	
making beds		taking out the trash	

(a) Who helps with the most jobs? _____

(b) Which is your favorite job? _____

    Why?_____

(c) Which is your least favorite job? _____

    Why?_____

©World Teachers Press® ~ www.worldteacherspress.com

Indicator: Reflects on and writes about responsibilities family members have around the home.

My Favorite Family Day

What do you and your family like to do together?
Plan and write about a favorite family day you have spent or would like to spend.

1. **Color the day of the week it is on.**

Su	M	T	W	Th	F	Sa

3. **Do you need to travel?** Yes / No

   If so, write what transportation you will need to take.

   _____

5. **Write keywords to describe what you will be doing.**

   _____

   _____

   _____

7. **Use your plan to write the story of your favorite family day. Add a picture.**

   _____

   _____

   _____

   _____

   _____

2. **Color the kind of day it is.**

4. **Who is there?**

   _____

   _____

   _____

6. **Highlight any words that describe how this day made you feel. Add any others you need.**

   excited   happy   tired

Indicator: Plans and writes about a favorite family day.

Family Celebrations

My Family and Friends

1. **Brainstorm all the celebrations your family celebrates.**

2. **Choose from the words to describe how your family celebrates these occasions.**

   Add any others you need.

party   meal   music   decorations   special clothes

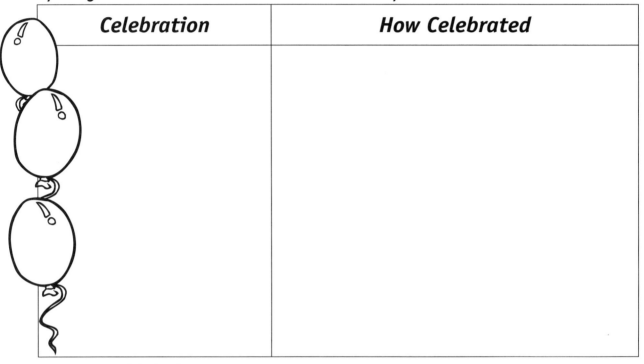

Celebration	How Celebrated

3. **Draw and label your family at your favorite celebration.**

4. **What is the most common family celebration in your class?**

_____

Indicator: Gains an understanding of different types of family celebrations and how they are celebrated.

©World Teachers Press® ~ www.worldteacherspress.com

Family Camping Vacation

This is a game for two to four players. You will need a counter each and a die. If you land on a square with a rope, climb up. If you land on a square with a muddy bank, slide down.

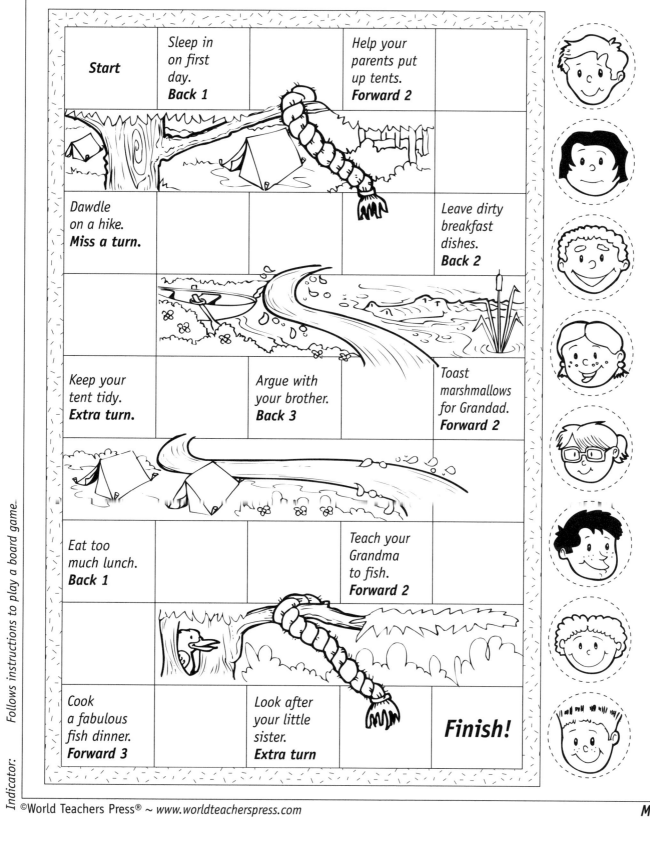

Start

Sleep in on first day. **Back 1**

Help your parents put up tents. **Forward 2**

Dawdle on a hike. **Miss a turn.**

Leave dirty breakfast dishes. **Back 2**

Keep your tent tidy. **Extra turn.**

Argue with your brother. **Back 3**

Toast marshmallows for Grandad. **Forward 2**

Eat too much lunch. **Back 1**

Teach your Grandma to fish. **Forward 2**

Cook a fabulous fish dinner. **Forward 3**

Look after your little sister. **Extra turn**

Finish!

Indicator: Follows instructions to play a board game.

©World Teachers Press® ~ www.worldteacherspress.com

What is a Friend?

A friend is someone you like who likes you too! Friends often have many things in common and like to do things together.

1. **Make checks or crosses on the chart to describe five of your friends.**

Name *(Intials only)*					
makes me laugh					
kind					
happy					
talkative					
shares					

2. **What things did most of your friends have in common?**

_____

3. **Design a "friendship" card to give to one of your friends.**

	Dear _____ , *This friendship card is just for you! You are a good friend because …*

©World Teachers Press® ~ www.worldteacherspress.com

My Birthday Party

Imagine you are allowed to plan your next birthday party. Think about what you and your friends like to do to answer the questions.

1. **Make a list of three people you will invite.**
   Next to each person's name, write something you like about him or her.

   Hayley   *She is a friendly person.*

   _____

   _____

   _____

2. **Where will your party be?** _____

   Why did you choose this place? _____

   _____

3. **Choose three foods you will have.**

   _____

   _____

4. **List some games and music your friends would like.**

   Games _____

   _____

   _____

   Music _____

5. **Draw you and your friends at the party.**

Indicator: Plans a party based on friends' likes and dislikes.

©World Teachers Press® ~ www.worldteacherspress.com

Me! ~ 43

Me!

Suggestions for use: Self-portrait drawings; collage seasonal clothing; label body parts; write information or poetry about "me" inside or around shape; add speech or thought bubbles.

©World Teachers Press® ~ www.worldteacherspress.com

- **Decorate each face with things about you.**

  Example:

  name

  photo

  favorite food

  friends

  talents

  nationality

- **Cut out template and construct a cube by folding along solid lines and gluing flaps.**

- **Hang from one corner on a piece of string to display.**

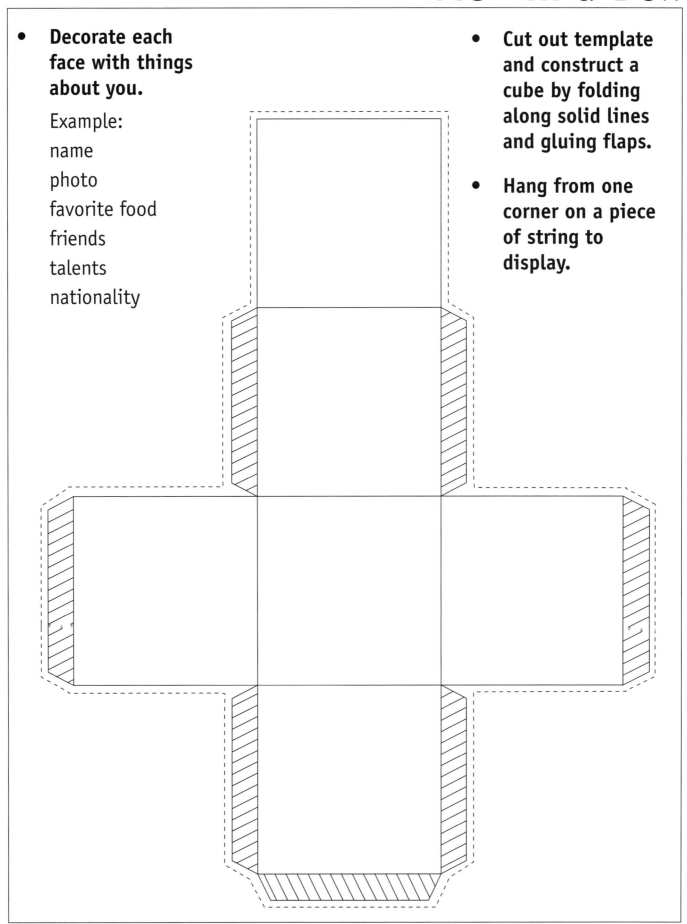

Answers

Answers for pages not listed need to be checked by the teacher.

Page 14 Our Five Senses

1. eye – see, ear – hear, nose – smell, tongue – taste, hand – touch

Page 15 My Eyes

1. Possible answers – scooter, smile, seesaw, seagull, sand, seaweed, sunscreen, splash, sandcastle, swim, sandwich, sunglasses, skipping rope, sunhat

2. Possible answers – key, bee, frisbee, tree

3. Possible answers – fish, dish, brush, bush, splash

4. Possible answers – frisbee, frog, friends, fruit

5. The mouse is peeking out of one of the sandcastles

Page 18 My Tongue

1. Sour – lemon, vinegar

    Sweet – gelatin crystals, sugar, chocolate, jam

    Salty – potato chip, peanuts, soy sauce

Page 19 My Hands

1. Possible answers – cotton balls/fluffy, sand/dry, honey/sticky, stick/pointy, golf ball/hard, water/wet, sandpaper/rough, cheek/soft

Page 27 Family Words

1. grandparents, grandchild

2. Possible answers – granddaughter, grandmother, grandfather

3. (a) husband   (b) sister   (c) uncle   (d) daughter

4. (a) wife   (b) daughter   (c) niece   (d) son

Page 28 Different Families

	My Family	*Keenan*	*Jacob*
number of people	Answers will vary	5	5
size of home	Answers will vary	small house	huge house
type of family	Answers will vary	noisy, busy	exciting
do together	Answers will vary	play music	ride horses

©World Teachers Press® ~ www.worldteacherspress.com